THE WASHINGTON BEEKEEPER

William Falconburg

CONTENTS

INTRODUCTION

Beekeeping in Washington State comes with its own unique challenges. Cold weather is only part of the equation. Moisture, fog, long periods of rain, hornets, difficult terrain, and inconsistent nectar flows can all have serious effects on colony health and survival. Many methods that work well in other parts of the country simply do not translate cleanly to western Washington conditions.

As a 3rd generation beekeeper, I grew up hearing about bees from both my mother and grandfather, who kept bees in California for many years. Later, after spending years studying bees and insects on my own, I eventually began raising honey bees here in Washington State and quickly discovered that keeping bees here required a very different approach.

This book is not meant to be an academic deep dive into every aspect of beekeeping. Instead, it is a practical introduction focused on helping beginners understand how bees function, what challenges they face in Washington, and how to avoid some of the common mistakes that can destroy colonies.

One of the most important things I have learned over the years is that bees do not need perfect conditions to survive.

They simply need stable conditions and a beekeeper willing to pay attention. Observation matters far more than perfection. The bees are constantly adapting to the environment around them, and successful beekeeping often comes down to understanding what the colony is trying to do and helping them do it more effectively.

Throughout this book I will be sharing both practical information and personal experiences gathered from working with bees in Washington's wet and unpredictable climate. Some of these ideas may differ from mainstream approaches, but everything presented here comes from direct observation, experience, and a genuine desire to help both bees and beekeepers succeed.

Whether you are planning to keep a single garden hive or eventually expand into a larger apiary, I hope the information in this book helps you better understand your bees, avoid unnecessary losses, and enjoy the process of working with one of the most fascinating creatures on earth.

Best of fortune with your beekeeping adventure.

MY EXPERIENCE

I am a 3rd generation beekeeper, and some of my earliest memories involving bees came from conversations with my mother and grandfather. Both kept bees in California for many years, and growing up I heard stories about colonies, honey production, hive construction, swarms, and the endless strange situations that seem to follow beekeepers around.

My grandfather built much of his own equipment by hand. Many of our conversations started in his wood shop while working on various woodworking projects and eventually drifted toward the bees. Looking back, I probably learned more during those casual conversations than I realized at the time.

My mother approached bees from a slightly different angle, usually through stories about managing colonies and the practical realities of maintaining apiaries. Between the two of them, bees were simply always present in my life in one form or another.

As I got older, my interest gradually shifted beyond basic beekeeping and more toward the bees themselves. I spent years studying:

- bee behavior
- colony organization
- insect biology
- predator relationships
- and environmental interactions

Even then, there is a major difference between studying bees and actually keeping them.

Eventually, after many years away from active beekeeping, I decided to begin raising honey bees myself here in Washington State. Almost immediately I realized that many of the assumptions and methods I had heard about from California beekeeping did not translate perfectly to western Washington conditions.

Washington presented entirely different challenges.

The biggest surprise was moisture.

My first bee yard looked excellent during the

afternoon. It had:

- good forage
- decent shelter
- nearby water
- and what appeared to be reasonable terrain

Unfortunately, I had unknowingly placed the colonies directly inside a heavy fog channel.

Nearly every morning the colonies were soaked in moisture. The hives stayed damp for long periods, mold developed rapidly, and the bees struggled badly. By the end of winter I had lost over half my colonies.

It was a painful lesson, but also an extremely valuable one.

That experience completely changed how I evaluated hive locations. I began paying far more attention to:

- airflow
- elevation
- moisture movement
- fog settlement
- drainage
- and winter ventilation

The following year I relocated the colonies to a higher elevation on a different property.

This location was:

- closer to the top of a hill
- naturally shielded from wind
- surrounded by strong forage sources
- and significantly drier overall

The improvement was dramatic.

At the same time, the new location introduced entirely different problems.

The property was gated, which improved security, but access became difficult because I depended on the property owner's operating hours to reach the bees. The location was also roughly an hour from my home, making inspections and emergency work much harder.

That experience taught me another important lesson:
a perfect bee yard on paper is not always practical in reality.

Over the years I have dealt with:

- moisture problems
- hornets
- ants
- rodents
- difficult terrain
- poor access

- winter losses
- swarming
- weak queens
- and all the countless unpredictable issues that eventually challenge every beekeeper

One thing I have learned for certain is that beekeeping never truly becomes "solved."

Just when you think you understand everything happening inside a colony, the bees —or the environment around them—will introduce some completely new problem that forces you to adapt and learn again.

Oddly enough, that is part of what makes beekeeping so enjoyable.

There is always more to observe.
Always more to understand.
Always another challenge waiting.

Keeping bees in Washington can absolutely be difficult at times, especially for beginners, but it is also deeply rewarding. Watching a healthy colony survive winter, expand during spring, and thrive through the nectar flow creates a level of satisfaction that is difficult to explain to someone who has never worked with bees.

You will make mistakes.

Every beekeeper does.

The important thing is to:

- pay attention
- learn from failures
- stay adaptable
- and continue improving your understanding of the bees and the environment around them

Honey bees are incredibly important creatures, and every responsible beekeeper helping maintain healthy colonies contributes something valuable to the world around them.

I sincerely hope the information in this book helps you avoid some of the mistakes I made, better understand your own bees, and enjoy the experience of beekeeping as much as I have.

Best of fortune with your own beekeeping adventure.

HIVE BASICS

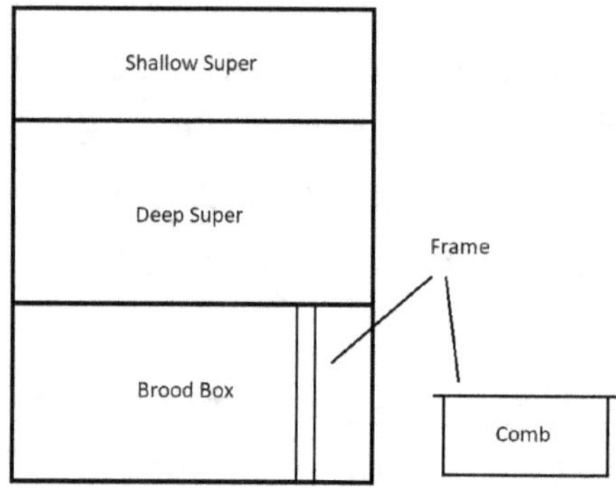

Before getting into hive management, mites, swarms, or honey production, it is important to understand how a colony actually functions. Many beginner problems happen because people look at a hive as a box full of individual bees instead of a single organized living system.

A honey bee colony is best understood as a superorganism. Individual bees matter, but the colony itself is the true living unit. Every bee inside the hive has a purpose, and the survival of the colony depends on thousands of bees constantly communicating and adapting to changing conditions.

Honey bees live in colonies that can range from only a few thousand bees during winter to well over fifty thousand during peak spring and summer populations. Inside the colony there are three primary types of bees: workers, drones, and the queen.

Workers are female bees and make up the overwhelming majority of the colony. They perform nearly every task required for survival. Workers clean the hive, feed brood, build comb, guard the entrance, regulate temperature, collect nectar and pollen, process honey, and defend the colony from threats.

Drones are the male bees. Their primary purpose is reproduction. Unlike workers, drones do not gather food or produce wax. During spring and summer they are present because they are needed for breeding. As winter approaches and resources become scarce, the workers usually force the drones out of the hive to reduce food consumption.

Then there is the queen.

Despite the name, the queen does not truly "rule" the colony in the way most people imagine. The workers ultimately control the direction of the hive. The queen's primary role is egg laying and pheromone production. These pheromones help organize colony behavior and maintain stability within the hive.

If the queen becomes weak, injured, genetically undesirable, or too old, the workers will replace her without hesitation. Honey bee colonies are extremely practical. The survival of the colony always comes before the survival of any individual bee, including the queen herself.

Communication is one of the most fascinating aspects of bee behavior. Bees constantly exchange information using pheromones, vibration, physical contact, and movement patterns commonly referred to as dances. Through this communication the colony rapidly adapts to changing conditions.

For example:

- increasing nectar storage during heavy bloom periods
- shifting workers into defensive roles during attacks
- regulating brood production
- responding to temperature and moisture changes
- preparing for swarming

The speed and efficiency of this communication is what allows colonies to survive in difficult environments.

Most beginner hives in Washington will use a Langstroth hive system, so that is the system I will reference throughout this book. A standard Langstroth hive is built from stacked wooden boxes containing removable frames.

The bottom section is usually the brood box. This is where the queen lays eggs and where most brood production occurs. Above the brood box are additional boxes commonly called supers. These are primarily used for honey storage.

Inside each box are frames. The bees build comb onto these frames using wax they produce themselves. The comb is used to store honey and pollen while also providing space for raising brood.

The removable frame system is one of the most important developments in modern beekeeping because it allows the beekeeper to inspect the colony without completely destroying the hive structure. Frames can be removed individually to check:

- brood health
- food stores
- population growth
- queen activity
- disease
- mite levels
- honey production

When a new colony is introduced into a hive, either through a package, nuc, or swarm, the bees immediately begin establishing the brood area and drawing comb. Once the brood box becomes established, the colony gradually expands upward into additional boxes for food storage.

One of the most important things for a beginner to understand is that bees are not static creatures. Colonies are constantly changing. Population size, brood production, temperament, food storage, and defensive behavior can all shift dramatically depending on season, weather, food availability, predators, and colony health.

Successful beekeeping is not about forcing bees into a rigid system. It is about observing what the colony is trying to do and adjusting your management in ways that support healthy colony behavior.

The bees already know how to be bees.

Our job is to give them the best possible chance to succeed.

HIVE LOCATION

Where you place your bees will have a massive effect on colony health, honey production, winter survival, and the amount of work required to keep the colonies alive. A good location can make average colonies perform well, while a poor location can destroy even strong colonies.

One of the biggest mistakes beginners make is assuming bees can successfully live anywhere. While honey bees are highly adaptable, some locations create so many problems that keeping bees there becomes impossible.

The goal is not to find a perfect location. Perfect locations rarely exist. Instead, you want a location where the advantages outweigh the problems and where the negative factors can be reasonably managed.

If possible, always maintain access to more

than one location where bees can be kept. Having an alternate location available can be extremely valuable for:

- making splits
- isolating weak colonies
- relocating aggressive bees
- swarm management
- emergency situations
- managing mite issues

Even a temporary backup location can save colonies when unexpected problems arise.

FOOD SOURCES

Food availability is one of the first things you should evaluate when selecting a bee yard location. Bees require large amounts of nectar and pollen throughout spring and summer in order to build healthy populations and store enough food for winter.

When scouting a location, pay attention to:

- flowering trees
- blackberry patches
- clover
- wildflowers
- gardens
- agricultural crops
- natural forest growth

Also pay attention to what blooms at different times of year. A location may look fantastic during one month and then become nearly barren during the rest of the season.

One important thing beginners often misunderstand is that your garden will not be the bees' only food source. Honey bees regularly travel several miles while foraging. Your flowers help, but the surrounding environment matters far more than a single garden. Additionally, you may feel like they are completely ignoring your flowers or garden but the truth is they are not. They may have a higher value food source they are hitting hard and may get to yours later or they maybe simply be tasking a smaller amount of bees to your plants that are gathering while you aren't watching them.

WATER SOURCES

Bees absolutely require water, but too much moisture can become a serious problem, especially in Washington State. Poor moisture management kills many more colonies here than cold temperatures do.

Standing water should be approached carefully. Slow moving or stagnant ponds can create several problems:

- excessive humidity
- bacteria growth
- mosquito populations
- hornet activity
- drowning risks

Clean flowing water is generally much safer than stagnant water.

After heavy rains, pay attention to where water collects and how it moves through the property. Areas that remain wet for long periods can dramatically increase moisture problems inside the hive.

TERRAIN AND MOISTURE FLOW

Terrain matters far more than many people realize.

Cold air, fog, and moisture naturally settle into low areas. A location that looks perfectly fine during the afternoon may become completely saturated with fog and moisture during the early morning hours.

Avoid placing colonies in valleys or low spots whenever possible. Excess moisture forces the bees to spend enormous amounts of energy regulating humidity inside the hive and can lead to mold growth and winter losses.

At the same time, placing colonies fully exposed on top of a hill can create wind problems.

Ideally, hives should be placed:

- above heavy moisture settlement zones
- below extreme wind exposure
- on well-draining ground
- somewhere with steady airflow

In Washington, airflow and moisture control are often more important than temperature.

WIND AND SHELTER

Strong wind can stress colonies year-round and create major winter problems.

Providing some type of windbreak is extremely helpful. Trees, fencing, sheds, and natural terrain features can all reduce wind exposure without completely trapping moisture.

One of the best setups is a partially sheltered area that:

- blocks direct wind
- allows airflow
- prevents standing moisture
- keeps rain from constantly soaking the hive

equipment

If water is draining away from the colonies instead of through them, and the wind is moving past the hives instead of directly into them, you are already solving several major problems.

PREDATORS AND OTHER ANIMALS

Always evaluate the local animal population before placing colonies.

Not all animals are problems. Bumble bees and mason bees are usually beneficial and help indicate that the environment already supports pollinators. Likewise, these types of pollinators should not be counted against the food supply in the area. Even if bumble bees and mason bees saturated an area, they would not consume even a fraction of the food that a single honey bee hive would.

Other animals require more attention.

Hornets, ants, rodents, raccoons, and bears can all create serious issues depending on your location. One motivated bear can destroy an entire bee yard in a single night.

The presence of predators does not automatically mean a location is unusable, but it does mean you need a management plan before problems occur.

CHEMICAL EXPOSURE

Chemical exposure is often difficult to identify because the source may not be on your own property.

Nearby:

- agriculture
- forestry operations
- landscaping
- weed control
- mosquito spraying
- garden pesticides

can all affect colony health.

Even heavily forested locations are not necessarily safe. Many forestry operations use pesticides and herbicides as part of land management practices.

Whenever possible:

- speak with nearby landowners
- ask what chemicals are being used
- pay attention to spraying schedules
- avoid direct exposure routes

Also take a careful look at the chemicals you

personally use around your home and garden.

Often, small changes in timing or application methods can significantly reduce risk to the bees.

ACCESSIBILITY

One of the most overlooked parts of hive placement is simple access.

A beautiful location is not very useful if reaching the colonies becomes difficult.

Try to keep colonies reasonably close to home, especially as a beginner. Long travel times make inspections, feeding, swarm management, and emergency responses much harder.

If the colonies are kept on someone else's property:

- make sure access is reliable
- understand gate policies
- confirm you can enter when needed
- plan for after-dark access if emergencies occur

Missing the proper timing for certain hive tasks can have serious consequences.

FINAL THOUGHTS

Most bee yard problems cannot be completely eliminated, but they can usually be reduced through good planning and observation.

- stable conditions
- manageable moisture
- adequate food
- reasonable protection
- and a beekeeper paying attention to what the environment is doing around them.

A well-managed location will almost always outperform a "perfect" location that is poorly understood.

THE GARDEN HIVE

Over the last several years there has been a major increase in interest surrounding self-sufficiency, gardening, food production, and pollinator health. As a result, many people have become interested in keeping a small backyard hive.

Personally, I think that is a good thing.

The more people who learn about bees and help maintain healthy colonies, the better. Even a single well-managed hive can make a meaningful difference for local pollination and help people develop a stronger understanding of the natural systems around them.

That being said, starting a garden hive successfully requires more than simply buying a box of bees and placing them near some flowers.

A successful garden hive depends on three primary elements:

- understanding
- equipment
- bees

Of these three, understanding is by far the most important.

LEARN BEFORE YOU BUY

One of the biggest beginner mistakes is purchasing equipment and bees before learning how colonies function.

Study first.

Learn about:

- colony structure
- seasonal behavior
- nectar flows
- brood development
- swarming
- winter challenges
- moisture management
- common predators
- food sources in your area

The more you understand before getting bees, the easier your first year will be.

You do not need to become an expert before starting, but basic preparation makes a huge difference.

UNDERSTAND YOUR LOCAL ENVIRONMENT

Your garden is only one small part of the bees' environment.

Honey bees forage over large areas and may travel several miles searching for nectar and pollen. Pay attention not only to your own yard, but also:

- nearby trees
- gardens
- blackberry patches
- wildflowers
- agricultural land
- forest growth
- neighboring landscaping

Also pay attention to what blooms during different times of year.

A location that looks amazing during spring may become a food desert by late summer.

KEEP YOUR FIRST SETUP SIMPLE

Many beginners become fascinated by the huge variety of hive designs available:

- Langstroth
- Top Bar
- Warre
- Skep
- horizontal hives
- flow hives
- and countless custom variations

Experimentation is fine later on.

For your first hive, simplicity is your friend.

Different hive styles often require different management methods. Trying to learn multiple systems at once creates unnecessary confusion and increases the chances of making serious mistakes.

Pick one system and learn it well before expanding into others.

For this book, I will primarily reference the standard Langstroth hive because it is the most common system in Washington and generally the easiest for beginners to find equipment and support for.

BASIC EQUIPMENT

For a basic garden hive you will generally need:

- brood box
- honey super

- bottom board
- inner cover
- outer cover
- frames and foundation
- feeder
- hive tool
- smoker
- bee suit or protective gear
- sugar water spray bottle

Some people insist that smokers, suits, or spray bottles are unnecessary. Experienced beekeepers can often work without them, but for beginners these tools are extremely helpful and can make the learning process far less stressful.

As your confidence and experience grow, you can decide which tools fit your own management style.

OPTIONAL EQUIPMENT

There are also many optional upgrades and variations available:

- screened bottom boards
- frame grips
- frame rests
- telescoping covers
- entrance reducers
- moisture quilts

- alternate foundation types

These can all be useful, but beginners should avoid overcomplicating the hive during the first season.

Learn the basics first.

Once you understand normal colony behavior, experimentation becomes much easier and much safer for the bees.

PACKAGES VS NUCS

Before getting bees, spend time learning the difference between:

- packages
- nucs

Both can work well, but they behave very differently during establishment.

Packages are essentially artificial swarms placed into a new hive. They require the bees to fully establish the colony from scratch.

Nucs are small functioning colonies that already contain:

- brood
- drawn comb
- food stores
- and an accepted queen

Because nucs are already partially established, they are often easier for beginners to manage successfully.

INSTALLING YOUR BEES

Once your equipment is assembled and your bees arrive, try to get them settled into the hive calmly and efficiently.

If starting with packages:

- begin feeding immediately
- reduce unnecessary disturbance
- allow the bees time to settle

Early feeding helps encourage the bees to:

- remain in the hive
- begin drawing comb
- establish brood quickly

A completely empty hive does not smell like home to the bees. Freshly installed packages sometimes abscond because they do not yet recognize the hive as a secure location.

One drawn frame from an existing colony can dramatically improve acceptance because it tells the bees:

"Other bees have successfully lived here before."

DON'T OVERFEED

Sugar water is useful during initial establishment, but beginners often continue feeding for too long.

If overfed, bees may begin storing sugar syrup as honey instead of gathering natural nectar.

The goal of early feeding is simply to help the colony get established and drawing comb—not to replace natural foraging entirely.

Once the bees are actively building comb and bringing in resources on their own, feeding should usually be reduced or stopped.

OBSERVE YOUR BEES

One of the most valuable things a beginner can do is simply watch the hive.

Pay attention to:

- flight activity
- pollen collection
- temperament
- flight direction
- nectar flow timing
- weather response

Try to notice where the bees are traveling and what plants they are using throughout the season.

Do not be surprised if the bees seem more interested in distant blackberry patches than the flowers directly beside the hive. Bees prioritize efficiency and resource quality over human expectations.

FINAL THOUGHTS

A small garden hive can be an incredibly rewarding experience.

You will make mistakes.
Every beekeeper does.

The goal is not perfection.

The goal is to learn how the colony behaves, understand what the bees are trying to accomplish, and gradually improve your ability to support them over time.

If you stay observant, avoid unnecessary complications, and remain willing to learn, even a single garden hive can teach you an enormous amount about bees, nature, and the environment around you.

SWARMS

Few things excite beekeepers more than seeing a swarm hanging from a tree branch.

To most people, a swarm looks dangerous and chaotic. In reality, swarming is one of the most natural and important parts of honey bee life. It is how colonies reproduce, expand their population, relocate, and in many cases improve their overall health.

For beekeepers, swarms can also be an excellent source of free bees.

WHAT IS A SWARM?

A swarm occurs when part of a colony leaves the hive along with a queen in order to establish a new colony elsewhere.

This usually happens during periods of:

- strong nectar flow
- rapid population growth
- overcrowding
- heavy brood production

As the colony grows, the bees eventually begin preparing replacement queens. Once new queens are nearly ready, the old queen often leaves the hive with a large group of workers.

That departing group becomes the swarm.

Contrary to popular belief, swarming is not necessarily a sign of failure or poor colony health. In many cases, strong healthy colonies are actually the most likely to swarm.

WHY SWARMS LOOK AGGRESSIVE

Swarms tend to frighten people because thousands of bees suddenly appear flying through the air all at once.

Fortunately, swarming bees are usually far less defensive than established colonies.

The swarm has:

- no brood to defend
- no honey stores to protect
- no permanent home yet established

Their primary focus is finding a new location to live, not attacking people.

That does not mean swarms should be handled carelessly, but they are often surprisingly calm compared to a fully established hive.

TEMPORARY CLUSTERING

After leaving the original hive, the swarm will often gather temporarily on:

- tree branches
- fences

- shrubs
- buildings
- vehicles
- or other elevated surfaces

This temporary cluster allows scout bees time to search for a suitable permanent home.

While scouts search, the main swarm remains grouped together around the queen. During this stage, the bees may remain in one location for several hours or even several days before moving on.

This is often the easiest time for beekeepers to collect them.

CATCHING SWARMS

There are many different methods used to catch swarms. Some are simple and effective. Others are unnecessarily complicated.

Personally, I prefer practical low-effort systems.

Swarm catching should not require:

- elaborate structures
- dangerous climbing
- excessive equipment
- or expensive setups

Simple usually works best.

One of the easiest approaches is placing swarm boxes around your apiary or in locations where bees are likely to travel.

A basic swarm box can be:

- an old hive body
- a nuc box
- or even a simple wooden box large enough to attract scouts

The bees are primarily searching for:

- shelter
- security
- appropriate internal space
- and a dry stable environment

SWARM BOX PLACEMENT

Randomly placing swarm boxes can still work, but strategic placement dramatically improves success rates.

Good locations often include:

- near existing apiaries
- along tree lines
- near nectar-heavy areas
- sheltered edges of clearings
- elevated locations with moderate protection

Height also matters.

Many successful swarm traps are placed roughly:

- 6 to 10 feet above ground

This tends to attract scout bees while still allowing reasonably safe retrieval.

That said, practicality matters. A swarm box twenty feet up a tree may attract bees, but retrieving a fully established colony from that height quickly becomes unpleasant.

The best swarm setups balance:

- accessibility
- visibility to scout bees
- shelter
- and ease of retrieval

USING DRAWN COMB

One of the best ways to improve swarm trap success is using old drawn comb.

A box that smells like bees is far more attractive than brand new equipment.

Even a single old frame can make a huge difference because it signals to scout bees that:

- the location has previously supported a colony
- the space is likely safe

- and conditions are acceptable for occupation

This is one reason older equipment often catches swarms more effectively than freshly assembled boxes.

PASSIVE SWARM CATCHING

You do not necessarily need to actively hunt swarms in order to benefit from them.

Many beekeepers simply place a few empty boxes around their apiary and allow nature to do the work.

This passive approach can:

- recover your own swarms
- capture feral swarms
- increase colony count
- and provide backup colonies after winter losses

Even a few swarm boxes placed strategically around your bee yard can produce surprisingly good results over time.

SWARMS VS EXTRACTING COLONIES

New beekeepers often confuse swarm catching with colony extraction.

These are very different activities.

Swarm catching involves collecting bees that are temporarily clustered and searching for a home.

Extractions involve removing fully established colonies from:

- walls
- roofs
- sheds
- crawl spaces
- chimneys
- or other structures

Once bees have built comb inside a structure, the process becomes significantly more difficult and usually requires specialized tools and experience.

Showing up expecting to collect a simple swarm only to discover bees established deep inside a wall can become a very long day.

SHOULD YOU ALLOW SWARMING?

Many beekeepers work aggressively to prevent swarming entirely.

Personally, I believe swarming serves important biological functions for honey bees.

Swarming naturally:

- interrupts brood cycles
- reduces overcrowding
- disperses genetics
- and can help reduce parasite pressure

That does not mean uncontrolled swarming is always desirable, especially in urban environments, but treating swarming as purely negative often ignores the natural role it plays in colony health and reproduction.

In many cases, good swarm management is more useful than complete swarm suppression.

FINAL THOUGHTS

Swarms are one of the most fascinating aspects of beekeeping.

For beginners, they can seem intimidating at first. Over time, many beekeepers begin to see them differently—not as a disaster, but as an opportunity.

A healthy respect for swarming behavior helps beekeepers better understand:

- colony growth
- reproduction

- seasonal behavior
- and how bees naturally adapt to their environment

Whether you actively pursue swarms or simply keep a few swarm boxes nearby, understanding swarm behavior is an important part of becoming a successful beekeeper.

PACKAGES AND NUCS

One of the first major decisions a new bee-keeper must make is how to get their bees.

For most beginners, this usually comes down to two primary options:

- packages
- nucs

Both can successfully establish healthy colonies, but they function very differently and each comes with its own advantages and disadvantages.

Understanding those differences before purchasing bees can save a great deal of frustration during your first season.

WHAT IS A PACKAGE?

A bee package is essentially an artificial swarm created by a beekeeper.

Package producers collect worker bees from multiple colonies and place them into a ventilated shipping container along with:

- a feeder can
- a separately caged queen
- and several pounds of worker bees

Most packages contain roughly:

- 2 to 4 pounds of bees
- or approximately 7,000 to 15,000 workers

The queen included with the package is usually unrelated to the majority of the workers inside.

Because of this, the bees must gradually accept the queen after installation.

HOW PACKAGES ARE PRODUCED

Large-scale package production typically requires substantial colony numbers.

Workers are physically shaken or brushed from strong colonies into collection containers and then measured into package cages.

The process works surprisingly well, but it is undeniably stressful for the bees.

The workers become:

- disoriented
- separated from their original colony
- temporarily homeless
- and introduced to an unfamiliar queen

Once installed into a hive, the bees must quickly organize themselves, release and accept the queen, begin drawing comb, establish brood production, and build a functioning colony from scratch.

Packages are essentially being asked to rapidly transform themselves into a stable colony under completely artificial conditions.

ADVANTAGES OF PACKAGES

Despite the stress involved, packages offer several advantages.

Lower Cost

Packages are usually less expensive than nucs because they:

- require less equipment
- are easier to transport
- and can be produced in large numbers

Easier Shipping

Because packages are lightweight and compact, they are commonly shipped long distances.

This allows beginners to purchase bees even when local nuc producers are unavailable.

Clean Starting Point

Packages begin with completely fresh equipment and empty frames.

Some beekeepers prefer this because it reduces the risk of:

- old contaminated comb
- hidden disease
- excessive wax moth damage
- or unwanted hive pests arriving with used equipment

CHALLENGES WITH PACKAGES

Packages also come with some significant challenges, especially for beginners.

Slower Establishment

Because the bees must build everything from scratch, package colonies usually develop more slowly than nucs.

The bees must:

- draw comb
- establish brood
- accept the queen
- organize food storage
- and build population simultaneously

This creates a difficult early growth phase.

Queen Acceptance Risks

Since the queen is unfamiliar to the workers, there is always some risk that the bees may reject or kill her.

This is known as balling the queen.

Proper installation and allowing gradual release time helps reduce this risk.

Absconding

Packages are essentially homeless swarms placed into unfamiliar equipment.

If conditions are poor, the bees may decide to abandon the hive entirely.

This is one reason immediate feeding and minimizing disturbance are so important during installation.

WHAT IS A NUC?

A nuc, short for nucleus colony, is a small functioning colony already established on frames.

Unlike packages, nucs usually include:

- an actively laying queen
- brood in various stages
- food stores

- drawn comb
- and workers already functioning together as a colony

Most nucs are sold in:

- 5-frame boxes
- though larger sizes sometimes exist

From the bees' perspective, a nuc is not starting over from scratch. It is simply expanding into a larger home.

ADVANTAGES OF NUCS

For beginners, nucs are often easier and more forgiving than packages.

Faster Colony Development

Because the colony already contains:

- brood
- drawn comb
- and a functioning queen

population growth begins immediately.

The bees are already organized and operating normally.

Lower Absconding Risk

Nucs are far less likely to abandon the hive because:

- brood is already present

- the queen is established
- and the colony already considers itself "home"

Bees are extremely reluctant to abandon uncapped brood.

Better Early Stability

Nucs generally handle:

- weather fluctuations
- food shortages
- and beginner mistakes

better than packages do during early establishment.

This makes them particularly attractive for new beekeepers in Washington where spring conditions can change rapidly.

CHALLENGES WITH NUCS

Nucs are not perfect either.

Higher Cost

Nucs usually cost more because they require:

- drawn frames
- additional equipment
- longer production time
- and more colony resources

Equipment Quality Varies

Not all nuc producers maintain high standards.

Poorly managed nucs may contain:

- weak queens
- excessive mites
- poor brood patterns
- disease
- or insufficient populations

Always inspect nucs carefully when possible and purchase from reputable producers.

Comb Quality Matters

Because nucs include existing comb, the condition of that comb matters.

Old black comb, heavy contamination, or damaged frames can create future problems if introduced into your apiary.

OVERWINTERED NUCS

One of the best types of nucs available are overwintered nucs.

These are colonies that successfully survived winter before being sold.

Overwinter survival demonstrates several valuable traits:

- population stability
- winter hardiness

- local adaptability
- and queen performance

In Washington State, where winter moisture creates major colony stress, overwintered bees can provide a significant advantage.

PRODUCING YOUR OWN NUCS

Once a beekeeper gains experience, producing nucs becomes relatively straightforward.

Many beekeepers create nucs by:

- splitting strong colonies
- introducing queens
- allowing swarm colonies to establish
- or capturing swarms in nuc boxes

Small-scale nuc production can:

- replace winter losses
- expand apiaries
- or generate additional income

For many hobby beekeepers, nuc production eventually becomes more practical and sustainable than purchasing packages every year.

WHICH IS BETTER?

Neither packages nor nucs are universally superior.

The better choice depends on:

- budget
- experience level
- local availability
- climate
- and management goals

That said, for most beginners:

- nucs are generally easier
- packages are generally cheaper

If the budget allows it, many new beekeepers find nucs less stressful during the first season.

FINAL THOUGHTS

Whether you choose packages or nucs, the most important factor is not the bees themselves—it is how well the colony is managed after installation.

Healthy bees still require:

- good hive placement
- moisture control
- proper nutrition
- observation
- and reasonable management

Both packages and nucs can become excellent productive colonies when given stable conditions and attentive care.

The bees already know how to build a colony.

Our responsibility is to give them an environment where they can succeed.

WINTER CONSIDERATIONS

Winter is one of the most difficult periods for honey bee colonies in Washington State. Many colonies that appear healthy during late summer fail before spring arrives, and in most cases the problem is not simply cold temperatures.

Cold is a bee problem.

Moisture is a beekeeper problem.

Honey bees are remarkably good at generating heat. A healthy winter cluster can maintain survivable temperatures even during extremely cold weather. What bees struggle with is prolonged moisture, poor ventilation, mold growth, and damp conditions inside the hive.

In Washington, winter survival often depends less on keeping the bees warm and more on keeping them dry.

HOW BEES SURVIVE WINTER

As temperatures drop, the colony forms a winter cluster around the queen.

The bees group tightly together and generate heat by vibrating their flight muscles. Bees on the outer layer of the cluster act as insulation while bees inside rotate positions over time to conserve energy and maintain temperature.

During winter:

- brood production slows dramatically
- nectar collection stops
- population decreases
- and food consumption becomes extremely important

The colony survives almost entirely on stored honey and pollen until spring returns.

THE REAL THREAT: MOISTURE

One of the biggest beginner mistakes is focusing entirely on insulation while ignoring ventilation.

Warm moist air naturally rises through the hive. Without adequate ventilation, condensation forms inside the colony and begins dripping back down onto the bees.

Cold damp bees die quickly.

Even relatively mild winters can become deadly if the hive remains wet for extended periods.

Excess moisture contributes to:

- mold growth
- weakened bees
- spoiled pollen stores
- disease pressure
- chilled brood
- and colony collapse

In many cases, a dry cold hive is safer than a warm damp hive.

VENTILATION

Good winter ventilation is absolutely critical in Washington.

The goal is not to create strong drafts through the hive. The goal is controlled airflow that allows moisture to escape before condensation builds up inside the colony.

There are many ways beekeepers improve winter ventilation:

- notched inner covers
- upper entrances

- screened bottom boards
- moisture quilts
- ventilation shims
- slightly propped lids
- elevated hive stands

Different methods work better in different locations, so experimentation is important.

Personally, I prefer setups that:

- allow moisture to escape upward
- reduce water accumulation
- and maintain steady airflow without directly blasting cold wind into the colony

HIVE ELEVATION

Keeping hives off the ground makes a major difference in Washington conditions.

Ground moisture, standing water, and fog can dramatically increase humidity inside the hive.

Raising colonies:

- improves airflow
- reduces moisture wicking
- and helps prevent water accumulation

Even lifting colonies:

- 6 to 12 inches off the ground

can noticeably improve winter conditions.

Pallets, hive stands, concrete blocks, or wooden platforms all work well.

SHELTER FROM RAIN

One of the best things you can do for winter colonies is reduce direct rain exposure.

Constant rain saturation slowly introduces moisture into the hive equipment itself. Wet wood retains water, increases humidity, and makes temperature regulation harder for the bees.

Simple shelters can help tremendously:

- roof extensions
- lean-tos
- small sheds
- wind barriers
- or covered bee yards

The goal is not to completely seal the colonies away from airflow. The goal is simply reducing direct water exposure while still maintaining ventilation.

WIND MANAGEMENT

Strong winter wind can create stress on colonies by:

- increasing heat loss
- disrupting flight opportunities

- and making temperature regulation more difficult

Natural or artificial windbreaks can help reduce this problem.

Good wind protection may include:

- fences
- shrubs
- tree lines
- stacked materials
- or partial structures

At the same time, avoid completely trapping moisture around the hives.

Still air and trapped humidity can become just as dangerous as excessive wind.

WINTER FOOD STORES

Healthy colonies require adequate food stores going into winter.

A colony that runs out of honey before spring will starve even if every other condition is ideal.

During fall inspections, monitor:

- honey reserves
- colony size
- brood levels
- and overall population strength

Weak colonies often struggle to survive winter because they lack:

- sufficient population
- adequate food
- or enough healthy workers to maintain cluster temperature

In some situations, combining weak colonies before winter may improve survival chances.

SCREENED BOTTOM BOARDS

Screened bottom boards generate mixed opinions among beekeepers, but they can be useful in wet climates when managed properly.

Potential advantages include:

- improved airflow
- reduced moisture buildup
- less water pooling
- and some disruption of mite recovery

However, screened bottoms are not magic solutions.

Poorly managed airflow can still create problems, especially if strong wind moves directly through the hive during freezing conditions.

As with most winter management methods, results depend heavily on:

- local climate
- hive placement
- moisture conditions
- and overall colony strength

FALL POPULATION CHANGES

As nectar flow decreases and winter approaches, colonies naturally reduce population size in order to conserve resources.

This includes:

- reducing brood production
- removing drones
- and concentrating resources around winter survival

A smaller healthy winter colony is often stronger than an oversized colony struggling to feed excess mouths.

OBSERVE YOUR LOCATION

Winter management is highly dependent on location.

A setup that works perfectly:

- on dry eastern Washington land may fail completely:
- in a wet western Washington fog channel

Pay attention to:

- where fog settles
- how water drains
- wind direction
- humidity levels
- and how moisture behaves around the hives

Your environment will teach you more than any universal winter formula.

FINAL THOUGHTS

Successful wintering is rarely about one perfect trick or piece of equipment.

Usually, it comes down to:

- moisture management
- stable airflow
- healthy colony strength
- adequate food
- and good location selection

The bees already know how to survive winter.

Our role is to avoid placing unnecessary environmental pressure on them during one of the hardest periods of the year.

If you can keep the colonies:

- reasonably dry
- reasonably ventilated
- and reasonably fed

their chances of surviving into spring improve dramatically.

MITE ASSESSMENTS

Few subjects in beekeeping generate more debate than mites.

For many beekeepers, mites become the primary focus of colony management. Others barely think about them until colonies begin failing. The reality is that mites are absolutely a serious problem, but they are also only one part of overall colony health.

One of the biggest mistakes a beekeeper can make is focusing so heavily on mites that they ignore every other factor affecting the bees.

A colony struggling with:

- moisture
- starvation
- poor ventilation
- weak genetics
- pesticide exposure

- hornet pressure
- or poor nutrition

may collapse regardless of mite levels.

Before taking action, you must first make an honest assessment of the colony as a whole.

START WITH OBSERVATION

The first responsibility of a beekeeper is accurate observation.

Before reaching for treatments or management changes, stop and ask:

- What is actually happening in this colony?
- What problems are visible?
- What conditions are improving the colony?
- What conditions are hurting it?

Strong beekeeping starts with understanding the situation clearly—not reacting blindly.

A useful habit is creating two simple mental categories:

- What is helping the bees?
- What is hurting the bees?

Then prioritize accordingly.

COMPARE STRONG AND WEAK COLONIES

One of the best ways to evaluate colony health is comparison.

Look at:

- strong colonies
- weak colonies
- neighboring apiaries
- different locations
- seasonal differences

Pay attention to:

- brood patterns
- bee behavior
- food stores
- moisture conditions
- defensive behavior
- population size
- honey production
- and visible mite pressure

Ask yourself:

- What is different?
- What conditions appear stable?
- Which colonies are consistently thriving?

Sometimes the answer has little to do with mites at all.

UNDERSTAND WHAT MITES ACTUALLY DO

Varroa mites weaken colonies by feeding

on developing bees and spreading disease throughout the hive.

Heavy mite pressure often leads to:

- weakened workers
- poor brood health
- virus transmission
- reduced winter survival
- and eventual colony collapse

Healthy colonies can sometimes tolerate low mite populations for long periods, but unchecked mite growth eventually becomes extremely dangerous.

The challenge is finding management methods that reduce mite pressure without excessively harming the bees themselves.

THE PROBLEM WITH PURELY REACTIVE MANAGEMENT

Many beginner beekeepers panic the moment they hear the word "mites."

This often leads to a cycle of:

- constant treatments
- constant interventions
- and excessive hive disturbance

More management is not always better management.

Every time the hive is opened, disturbed, chemically altered, or forced into unnatural conditions, stress is added to the colony.

CHEMICAL TREATMENTS

Most mite treatments function by using chemicals or substances designed to kill mites faster than they harm bees.

The difficulty is obvious:
mites and bees are both arthropods living inside the same environment.

No treatment is completely free of tradeoffs.

Potential concerns may include:

- colony stress
- queen disruption
- brood impact
- residue buildup
- resistance development
- and repeated dependency

At the same time, completely ignoring heavy mite infestations can also destroy colonies.

This is why balanced observation matters more than ideological extremes.

The goal is understanding:

- colony condition
- environmental stress

- population strength
- seasonal timing
- and long-term colony stability

NON-CHEMICAL MANAGEMENT METHODS

Many beekeepers experiment with methods intended to reduce mite pressure while minimizing harm to the colony.

Some examples include:

- brood interruption
- drone brood removal
- screened bottom boards
- colony splitting
- encouraging swarming
- brood cycle management
- and selective breeding

None of these methods are perfect solutions by themselves, but many can contribute to lowering overall mite pressure when combined with strong colony management.

DRONE BROOD REMOVAL

Drone brood removal is one commonly discussed technique.

Varroa mites often prefer drone brood because drones remain capped longer during development, giving mites more time to reproduce.

Some beekeepers place drone comb frames into the hive, allow them to become heavily occupied, then remove and freeze the capped drone brood before returning the cleaned frame.

This physically removes a portion of the mite population from the colony.

The advantage is that it reduces mites without heavily exposing the colony to chemicals.

The disadvantage is that it requires:

- monitoring
- timing
- labor
- and consistency

Its effectiveness varies depending on colony conditions and overall management.

SWARMING AND BROOD INTERRUPTION

One thing that deserves serious consideration is the effect swarming has on mite reproduction.

Mites rely heavily on brood cycles in order to reproduce effectively.

During swarming:

- brood production is interrupted
- egg laying slows or temporarily stops
- and colony structure changes dramatically

This naturally disrupts mite reproduction. Completely suppressing all swarming behavior removes some of the colony's natural pressure-release mechanisms.

Swarming also places the bees into:

- increased grooming behavior
- high mobility
- and aggressive hive-cleaning activity

All of these factors may contribute to reducing mite pressure.

BREEDING AND RESILIENCE

Over time, colonies exposed to environmental pressure often develop varying levels of resilience.

Some colonies:

- groom mites more effectively
- detect damaged brood more efficiently
- or maintain stronger winter survival under pressure

Pay attention to which colonies consistently:

- survive winter
- recover quickly
- maintain strong brood patterns
- and function well under local conditions

Long-term colony strength often comes from selecting for stability and resilience—not simply short-term survival.

AVOID SINGLE-CAUSE THINKING

One of the most dangerous habits in beekeeping is assuming every problem has a single cause.

Mites matter.

But so do:

- nutrition
- genetics
- moisture
- pesticides
- forage quality
- environmental stress
- and management style

Colonies usually fail because of multiple overlapping pressures, not one isolated issue.

FINAL THOUGHTS

Mites are a serious challenge in modern bee-keeping and should never be ignored.

At the same time, panic, overreaction, and blind treatment cycles can create problems of their own.

Strong mite management begins with:

- careful observation
- realistic assessment
- stable colony conditions
- and understanding how bees naturally respond to stress

The healthiest colonies are usually not the colonies receiving the most interference.

They are the colonies living in stable conditions with a beekeeper who understands when to help, when to adjust conditions, and when to simply stay out of the bees' way.

THE SURPRISING TRUTH ABOUT HORNETS

The immediate assumption is usually: "Hornets are destroying my hives!"

While hornets absolutely can become a serious problem under certain conditions, the reality is far more complicated than many people realize.

In moderation, hornets are not simply mindless destroyers of bee colonies. They are part of the natural ecosystem surrounding the hive, and in some situations their presence may actually benefit overall colony health and behavior.

That does not mean hornets should be ignored entirely.

It means they should be understood realistically.

NOT ALL HORNET PRESSURE IS BAD

Predators are a normal part of nature.

Honey bees evolved alongside:

- hornets
- wasps
- ants
- spiders
- birds
- and countless other threats

A healthy colony is not designed to exist in complete isolation from predators. In fact, some level of environmental pressure often helps maintain stronger colony behavior.

Mild hornet activity can:

- increase defensive awareness
- stimulate guard behavior
- reduce colony complacency
- and pressure weaker bees out of the population

This does not mean hornets are "helping" bees intentionally. They are predators doing what predators do. But ecosystems are rarely as simple as:

"good species" versus "bad species."

TIMING MATTERS

One reason hornet pressure sometimes appears less catastrophic than beginners expect is seasonal timing.

In Washington, hornet populations often peak during late summer and early fall—roughly the same period when bee colonies naturally begin reducing population size before winter.

At this stage:

- nectar flow is slowing
- drones are being removed
- brood production is decreasing
- and colonies are becoming more selective about resource use

A healthy colony can often absorb minor losses during this period far more effectively than during spring buildup.

Weak colonies, however, may struggle badly under additional pressure.

HORNETS OFTEN TARGET WEAKER BEES

Like many predators, hornets frequently capture:

- slower bees
- injured bees
- aging workers
- isolated foragers
- or weakened individuals

Healthy fast-moving workers are much harder to catch consistently.

This selective pressure may indirectly contribute to stronger overall colony performance by removing bees already struggling with:

- injury
- disease
- pesticide exposure
- or age-related decline

Again, this does not make hornets "good."

It simply means nature often applies pressure unevenly.

COLONY BEHAVIOR CHANGES

One of the most interesting effects hornet activity can have is behavioral.

Colonies under mild predator pressure often become:

- more alert
- more defensive
- more responsive to intrusion

- and less tolerant of unwanted hive visitors

This can have several secondary effects.

Bees dealing with hornets may become less accepting of:

- robber bees
- ants
- scavenging insects
- and other small intruders

A hive under no pressure at all sometimes becomes surprisingly permissive toward pests and opportunistic insects.

OTHER HIVE INTRUDERS

Many insects attempt to exploit the warmth and protection of bee hives.

Some examples include:

- ants
- earwigs
- spiders
- wax moths
- small hive beetles
- and pill bugs

Not all of these creatures directly attack the bees, but many can:

- spread contamination
- damage comb
- consume resources

- or increase disease pressure

Colonies actively defending against hornets often become generally more aggressive toward all unwanted intruders.

BALANCE MATTERS

Too much hornet pressure absolutely becomes dangerous.

A weak colony overwhelmed by large numbers of hornets may:

- lose foragers rapidly
- struggle to defend entrances
- become stressed
- and fail before winter

The goal is understanding that mild natural pressure and total annihilation are not the same thing.

A balanced ecosystem usually contains predators.

BALD-FACED HORNETS

One species deserves special mention: the Bald-faced Hornet.

In my experience, these hornets are significantly more dangerous to honey bee colonies than many smaller local wasp and hornet species.

They are:

- larger
- stronger
- more aggressive
- and far more difficult for bees to stop once inside the hive

Smaller hornets may harass entrances and capture isolated workers, but Bald-faced Hornets can sometimes directly overpower defensive bees and move through colonies with surprisingly little resistance.

Unlike smaller predators that mostly target vulnerable bees outside the hive, Bald-faced Hornets may aggressively attack the colony itself.

For this reason, I generally tolerate mild activity from smaller hornet species while actively removing Bald-faced Hornet nests near my hives.

There is a major difference between:

- manageable environmental pressure and
- a predator the colony cannot realistically defend against.

DON'T STRESS OVER EVERY HORNET

A few hornets flying around does not automatically mean the colony is doomed.

Watch the bees carefully.

Ask:

- Are the bees still flying normally?
- Is the colony maintaining population?
- Are guard bees responding effectively?
- Is the pressure occasional or constant?
- Is the colony showing signs of collapse?

Healthy colonies are often far more resilient than beginners expect.

SUPPORT THE COLONY FIRST

If hornet pressure becomes excessive, focus first on strengthening the bees themselves.

Strong colonies defend themselves far better than weak colonies.

Good support may include:

- reducing moisture stress
- improving nutrition
- maintaining healthy population levels
- reducing unnecessary hive disturbance
- and narrowing entrances during heavy

pressure

Healthy bees solve many problems on their own.

FINAL THOUGHTS

Hornets are part of the environment honey bees evolved within.

They are not automatically:

- unstoppable monsters
- nor harmless background insects

They are predators, and like all predators they create both pressure and balance within the ecosystem.

Understanding that balance is more useful than reacting emotionally to every hornet near the hive.

A healthy colony living in stable conditions can usually tolerate far more natural pressure than many beginners realize.

The goal is not eliminating every challenge the bees face.

The goal is helping the colony remain strong enough to handle those challenges successfully.